Delicious suppers

Delicious
suppers

LOVE FOOD

Love Food ™ is an imprint of Parragon Books Ltd

Parragon
Queen Street House
4 Queen Street
Bath BA1 1HE, UK

Cover and internal design by Mark Cavanagh
Introduction by Bridget Jones
Photography by Don Last
Additional photography by Gunter Beer
Home Economist Christine Last

ISBN 978-1-4075-0124-6
Printed in China

Notes for the reader
• This book uses imperial, metric and US cup measurements. Follow the same units of measurements throughout; do not mix imperial and metric.
• All spoon measurements are level: teaspoons are assumed to be 5 ml and tablespoons are assumed to be 15 ml.
• Unless otherwise stated, milk is assumed to be low fat and eggs are medium. The times given are an approximate guide only.
• Some recipes contain nuts. If you are allergic to nuts you should avoid using them and any products containing nuts. Recipes using raw or very lightly cooked eggs should be avoided by infants, the elderly, pregnant women, convalescents, and anyone suffering from illness.

Contents

Suppers

Supper is less stuffy than formal eating, more relaxed and altogether more in keeping with today's busy lifestyles. It is modern eating at its best.

Contemporary suppers

With people leading busier lives, evening eating is more important but, with less time for preparation, food has to be faster and easier. More singles, couples without kids, and families snacking separately have influenced the way we eat. To counter the trend for eating junk food in front of a movie and dismissing meals, recent interest has centered on food for wellbeing, with more informal eating providing cool occasions for quality time with family or friends.

With everyone busy all week and weekends being pretty crowded too—supper has become more popular as the main meal of the day. Weekend cooking can be a leisure pursuit—checking out fresh produce from the deli counter and sharing the cooking over drinks during the evening.

One-pot meals

A couple of decades ago supper ideas were mainly based around meat-and-veg dishes—but there are now lots of options.

• Substantial soups with fish, seafood, chicken, meat or bean curd, and lots of chunky vegetables, rice, noodles, or pasta, can be flavored with fresh herbs or chiles. Cook them ahead and eat with home-made croutons or crusty bread for a warming and filling supper.
• Patchwork salads are the new one-pot winners. Mix crispy vegetables, hard-cooked eggs, canned pulses, juicy olives, and deli meats or cheese. Toss in freshly

juicy olives, and deli meats or cheese. Toss in freshly cooked rice, pasta, or potatoes for a hot-cold eating experience.

• Dressings have travelled from salad bowl to grilled fish, poultry, meat, griddled polenta, couscous or pasta, and steamed root vegetables.

• Sautés and stir-fries use quick-cook ingredients, which can be prepared at home or bought ready prepared. Add raw shrimp, or strips of poultry or meat. Sage and onion, lemon and thyme, or mustard and capers are great for quick-fried one-pot meals—the seasoning does not have to be South-east Asian.

What is in store?

Having a supply of canned and frozen ingredients is a prerequisite for throwing together healthy suppers in no time. Remember to re-stock as you use them.

• Canned navy beans, chickpeas, and red kidney beans go into soups, stir-fries, salads, dips and spreads.

• Toasted pine nuts or almonds, chopped walnuts or pecans, and roasted pumpkin seeds are useful for topping vegetables, salads, fruit, or yogurt.

• Use conserves and jelly to flavor plain yogurt, melt with a little fruit juice for dessert sauce, or to glaze plain griddled meats.

• Among frozen vegetables, include chopped bell peppers, succotash mix, broccoli, cut green beans, chopped spinach, and lima beans.

• Open freeze fine-cut strips of meat or poultry on trays lined with plastic wrap, then pack. Cook as much as needed from frozen.

• Frozen pita, naan, or split ciabatta breads, split English muffins, crumpets, split savory biscuits, and baked pizza bases make instant pizzas or bruschetta.

1

Quick Supper Solutions

serves 6

12 oz/350 g broccoli

1 leek, sliced

1 celery stalk, sliced

1 garlic clove, crushed

12 oz/350 g potato, diced

4 cups vegetable stock

1 bay leaf

freshly ground black pepper

crusty bread or toasted croutons, to serve

speedy broccoli soup

Cut the broccoli into florets and set aside. Cut the thicker broccoli stalks into ½-inch/1-cm dice and put into a large pan with the leek, celery, garlic, potato, stock, and bay leaf. Bring to a boil, then reduce the heat, cover, and let simmer for 15 minutes.

Add the broccoli florets to the soup and return to a boil. Reduce the heat, cover, and let simmer for an additional 3–5 minutes, or until the potato and broccoli stalks are tender.

Remove from the heat and let the soup cool slightly. Remove and discard the bay leaf. Purée the soup, in small batches, in a food processor until smooth.

Return the soup to the pan and heat through thoroughly. Season to taste with pepper. Ladle the soup into warmed bowls and serve at once with crusty bread or toasted croutons.

serves 4

2/3 cup plain yogurt

1 tbsp wholegrain mustard

pepper

10 oz/280 g cooked skinless, boneless chicken breast, diced

5 oz/140 g iceberg lettuce, finely shredded

3 oz/85 g cucumber, thinly sliced

2 celery stalks, sliced

1/2 cup black seedless grapes, halved

8 x 8-inch/20-cm soft flour tortillas or 4 x 10-inch/25-cm soft flour tortillas

chicken wraps

Combine the yogurt and mustard in a bowl and season to taste with pepper. Stir in the chicken and toss until thoroughly coated.

Put the lettuce, cucumber, celery, and grapes into a separate bowl and mix well.

Fold a tortilla in half and in half again to make a cone that is easy to hold. Half-fill the tortilla pocket with the salad mixture and top with some of the chicken mixture. Repeat with the remaining tortillas, salad, and chicken. Serve at once.

serves 4

5^1/$_2$ oz/150 g arugula leaves

2 celery stalks, trimmed and sliced

^{1}/$_2$ cucumber, sliced

2 scallions, trimmed and sliced

2 tbsp chopped fresh parsley

1 oz/25 g walnut pieces

12 oz/350 g boneless roast chicken, sliced

4^1/$_2$ oz/125 g bleu cheese, cubed

handful of seedless red grapes, cut in half (optional)

salt and pepper

for the dressing

2 tbsp olive oil

1 tbsp sherry vinegar

1 tsp Dijon mustard

1 tbsp chopped mixed herbs

chicken, cheese & arugula salad

Wash the arugula leaves, pat dry with paper towels, and put them into a large salad bowl. Add the celery, cucumber, scallions, parsley, and walnuts and mix together well. Transfer onto a large serving platter. Arrange the chicken slices over the salad, then scatter over the cheese. Add the red grapes, if using. Season well with salt and pepper.

To make the dressing, put all the ingredients into a screw-top jar and shake well. Alternatively, put them into a bowl and mix together well. Drizzle the dressing over the salad and serve.

serves 4

1 tbsp peanut oil

1/2 tsp chili powder, or to taste

2 garlic cloves, crushed

1/2 red cabbage, shredded

2 leeks, sliced thinly

1 orange bell pepper, sliced thinly

1 carrot, sliced thinly

1 zucchini, sliced thinly

12 oz/350 g pork tenderloin, cubed

cooked fettucine or vermicelli, to serve

quick pork & pasta stir-fry

Heat the oil in a wok or large skillet over medium heat and add the chili powder, garlic, and red cabbage. Stir-fry for 2–3 minutes.

Stir in the rest of the vegetables and cook for another 2 minutes. Add the meat, then increase the heat and stir-fry for 5 minutes, or until the pork is well cooked and the dish is piping hot.

Serve immediately over fettucine or vermicelli.

serves 4

5 tbsp butter

2 tbsp vegetable oil

1 lb/450 g onions, thinly sliced

scant 1 cup red wine

salt and pepper

4 minute or frying steaks

2/3 cup heavy cream

green salad, to serve

minute steaks with onion sauce

Melt 3 tablespoons of the butter with half the oil in a large pan over medium heat. Add the onions, cover, and cook, stirring occasionally, for 10–15 minutes until softened and light golden brown.

Add half the wine to the onions and season to taste with salt and pepper. Bring to a boil, then reduce the heat to low and cook for an additional 5–10 minutes until very soft.

Meanwhile, melt the remaining butter with the remaining oil in a large, heavy-bottom skillet over medium heat. When hot, add the steaks, and cook, turning once, for 30–45 seconds each side for rare or 1–1½ minutes each side for medium. Season to taste with salt and pepper.

Strain the cooked onions, reserve the liquid and divide among 4 warmed plates. Arrange the cooked steaks on top.

Add the remaining wine to the skillet in which the steaks were cooked and bring to a boil, stirring to deglaze by scraping any sediment from the bottom of the skillet. Stir in the reserved onion liquid and the cream and season to taste with salt and pepper. Return to a boil, then reduce the heat and let simmer for 1–2 minutes.

Spoon the sauce over the steaks and serve with a green salad.

serves 4

2 tenderloin steaks, about 6 oz/
175 g each and 1 inch/
2.5 cm thick

olive or corn-seed oil,
for brushing

pepper

1 tbsp wholegrain mustard

2/3 cup mayonnaise

1 tbsp lemon juice

1 lb 2 oz/500 g eating apples

4 celery stalks, thinly sliced

1/2 cup walnut halves,
broken into pieces

31/2 oz/100 g mixed salad
greens

crusty bread, to serve

steak waldorf salad

Heat a thick, cast-iron stove-top pan or heavy-bottom skillet
over medium heat. Brush each steak with oil and season to taste
with pepper. When the pan is hot, add the steaks to the pan
and cook for 6–7 minutes for rare or 8–10 minutes for medium,
turning the steaks frequently and brushing once or twice with
oil. Remove from the pan and set aside.

Meanwhile, stir the mustard into the mayonnaise. Put the lemon
juice into a large bowl. Peel and core the apples, then cut them
into small chunks and immediately toss in the lemon juice. Stir
in the mustard mayonnaise. Add the celery and walnuts to the
apple mixture and toss together.

Arrange the salad greens on 4 plates, then divide the apple
mixture between them. Very thinly slice the steaks, divide
among the plates and arrange on top of the salads. Serve at once
with crusty bread.

serves 8

melted butter, for brushing

4 lb/1.8 kg whole fresh salmon, dressed

salt and pepper

1 lemon, sliced

few sprigs of fresh parsley, plus extra to garnish

½ cup white wine or water

lemon wedges, to serve

for the quick hollandaise sauce

2 tbsp white wine vinegar

2 tbsp water

6 black peppercorns

3 egg yolks

9 oz/250 g unsalted butter

2 tsp lemon juice

salt and pepper

poached salmon with quick hollandaise sauce

Preheat the oven to 300°F/150°C. Line a large roasting tin with a double layer of foil and brush with butter. Season the salmon with salt and pepper, lay on the foil and place the lemon slices and parsley on top. Pour over the wine and gather up the foil to make a fairly loose package.

Bake for 50-60 minutes. Remove from the oven and leave to stand for 15 minutes before removing from the foil to serve hot.

Meanwhile, to make the hollandaise sauce, put the wine vinegar and water into a small pan with the peppercorns, bring to a boil, then reduce the heat and simmer until it is reduced to 1 tablespoon (take care, this happens very quickly). Strain. Mix the egg yolks in a food processor and add the strained vinegar while the machine is running.

Melt the butter in a small pan and heat until it almost turns brown. Again, while the food processor is running, add three-quarters of the butter, the lemon juice, then the remaining butter and season well with salt and pepper.

Turn the sauce into a serving bowl or keep warm for up to 1 hour in a bowl over a pan of warm water. To serve cold, allow to cool and store in the refrigerator for up to 2 days. Serve the sauce with the salmon, garnished with the parsley sprigs and lemon wedges.

serves 4

9 oz/250 g rice vermicelli noodles

2 tbsp sesame oil

6 scallions

6 oz/175 g white mushrooms

1/2 cucumber, cut into matchsticks

for the dressing

4 tbsp sesame oil

2 tbsp Thai fish sauce

juice of 2 limes

1 tsp sugar

1–2 tsp hot chili sauce

2 tbsp chopped fresh cilantro

hot & sour noodle & mushroom salad

Soak the noodles in a bowl of hot water for 10 minutes, or according to the package instructions. Drain and place in a large bowl. Add the sesame oil and toss until the noodles are coated with the oil.

Slice the scallions and mushrooms, then cut the cucumber into short thin sticks. Add to the noodles in the bowl.

To make the dressing, place the sesame oil, fish sauce, lime juice, sugar, and chili sauce in a small bowl and whisk together. Stir in the chopped cilantro.

Pour the dressing over the salad and toss until coated. Serve at once.

serves 4–6

6 large red, orange, or
yellow bell peppers, each cut
in half lengthwise, broiled,
and skinned

4 hard-cooked eggs, shelled

12 anchovy fillets in oil,
drained

12 large black olives, pitted

extra-virgin olive oil or
garlic-flavored olive oil,
for drizzling

sherry vinegar, to taste

salt and pepper

country-style crusty bread,
to serve

broiled bell pepper salad

Remove any cores and seeds from the broiled bell peppers and cut the flesh into thin strips. Arrange on a serving platter.

Cut the eggs into wedges and arrange over the bell pepper strips, along with the anchovy fillets and olives.

Drizzle oil over the top, then splash with sherry vinegar, adding both to taste. Sprinkle a little salt and pepper over the top and serve with crusty bread.

serves 4

4 red-fleshed sweet potatoes,
about 9 oz/250 g each

1 cup frozen fava beans

scant 3/4 cup frozen corn
kernels

4 oz/115 g fine long green
beans

1 tbsp olive oil

1 tbsp balsamic vinegar

freshly ground black pepper

5 oz/140 g tomatoes,
cut into small pieces

2 tbsp torn fresh basil leaves,
plus extra leaves to garnish

corn & green bean-filled baked sweet potatoes

Preheat the oven to 375°F/190°C. Scrub the sweet potatoes and pierce the skin of each potato with a sharp knife several times. Arrange on a baking sheet and bake in the preheated oven for 1–1¼ hours, or until soft and tender when pierced with the point of a sharp knife. Keep warm.

Meanwhile, bring a pan of water to a boil, add the fava beans and corn, and return to a boil. Reduce the heat, cover, and let simmer for 5 minutes. Trim the green beans, cut in half, and add to the pan. Return to a boil, then reduce the heat, cover, and let simmer for 3 minutes, or until the green beans are just tender.

Blend the oil with the vinegar in a small bowl and season to taste with pepper. Drain the corn and beans, return to the pan, add the tomatoes, and pour the dressing over. Add the torn basil leaves and mix well.

Remove the sweet potatoes from the oven, cut in half lengthwise, and open up. Divide the corn and bean filling among the potatoes and serve at once, garnished with basil leaves.

2

A Family Affair

serves 4

4 tbsp butter

1 onion, chopped

3 leeks, sliced

8 oz/225 g potatoes,
peeled and cut into
3/4-inch/2-cm cubes

3 cups vegetable stock

salt and pepper

2/3 cup light cream (optional)

2 tbsp snipped fresh chives,
to garnish

leek & potato soup

Melt the butter in a large pan over medium heat, add the vegetables and cook, stirring frequently, for 2–3 minutes until slightly softened. Pour in the stock and bring to a boil, then reduce the heat, cover and let simmer, stirring occasionally, for 15 minutes.

Remove from the heat and let cool slightly. Transfer the soup to a food processor and process until smooth. Return to the rinsed-out pan.

Reheat the soup, season to taste with salt and pepper, and serve in warmed bowls, garnished with swirls of cream, if desired, and chives.

serves 4

3 tbsp butter

4 shallots, chopped

1 leek, trimmed and sliced

1 lb/450 g skinless chicken breasts, chopped

2 1/2 cups chicken bouillon

1 tbsp chopped fresh parsley

1 tbsp chopped fresh thyme

salt and pepper

3/4 cup heavy cream

sprigs of fresh thyme, to garnish

cream of chicken soup

Melt the butter in a large pan over medium heat. Add the shallots and cook for 3 minutes, stirring and until slightly softened. Add the leek and cook for another 5 minutes, stirring. Add the chicken bouillon and herbs and season with salt and pepper. Bring to a boil, then lower the heat and simmer for 25 minutes, until the chicken is tender and cooked through. Remove from the heat and let cool for 10 minutes.

Transfer the soup into a food processor and process until smooth (you may need to do this in batches). Return the soup to the pan and warm over low heat for 5 minutes.

Stir in the cream and cook for another 2 minutes, then remove from the heat and ladle into serving bowls. Garnish with sprigs of thyme and serve.

serves 4

4 turkey breast fillet steaks,
about 5 oz/140 g each

1 tbsp red currant jelly

2 tbsp red wine vinegar

1 tbsp orange juice

freshly cooked green beans,
tossed in butter, with
8 oz/225 g halved cherry
tomatoes and 4 chopped
scallions, to serve

fresh red currants, to garnish
(optional)

for the bean purée

2 tbsp olive oil

1 lb 2 oz/500 g canned
cannellini beans, drained,
rinsed, and coarsely mashed

2–3 garlic cloves, crushed

1 tbsp chopped fresh mint

turkey steaks with bean purée

Wipe the turkey steaks with paper towels and put into a large, shallow dish. Heat the red currant jelly with the vinegar and orange juice in a small pan over low heat and stir until smooth. Once smooth, cover and allow the marinade to cool in the fridge, before pouring over the turkey and leaving to marinate for 30 minutes.

When ready to cook, heat a stove-top grill pan over high heat until almost smoking. Add the turkey and cook for 5–6 minutes on each side, or until cooked.

Meanwhile, mix all the ingredients for the bean purée together in a bowl, transfer to a nonstick pan over low heat and heat through, stirring frequently, for 6–7 minutes, or until piping hot. Alternatively, transfer the mixture to a microwavable container, cover with plastic wrap, and heat in a 1,000-watt microwave oven for 3–4 minutes. Remove and let stand for 2 minutes. Remove and discard the plastic wrap and stir well.

Serve the turkey steaks on the bean purée with freshly cooked green beans, tossed in butter, cherry tomatoes, and scallions and garnish with red currants, if desired.

serves 4

4 tbsp vegetable oil

2–3 large onions, thinly sliced

16 white mushrooms,
thinly sliced

2 cups freshly ground beef

salt and pepper

1 ciabatta loaf

4 tomatoes, sliced (optional)

1 cup red wine or beef stock

salisbury steak

Heat the oil in a skillet over high heat. Add the onions and mushrooms and cook quickly until soft. Push the vegetables to the side of the skillet.

Season the beef to taste with salt and pepper, then shape into four round patties. Add to the skillet and cook, in batches if necessary, until starting to brown, then carefully flip over and cook the other side. Cut the ciabatta in half then slice horizontally so that there are 4 pieces. Lightly toast the ciabatta pieces and divide among 4 plates. Top with the tomato slices, if using. Remove the meat patties from the skillet and set them on the ciabatta slices.

Bring the onions and mushrooms back to the center of the skillet, pour over the wine, and heat until boiling. Continue boiling for 1 minute, or until slightly reduced, then remove from the heat and spoon over the meat patties. Serve immediately.

serves 4

1 thick slice white bread,
crusts removed

3 cups freshly ground beef,
pork, or lamb

1 small egg

1 tbsp finely chopped onion

1 beef bouillon cube,
crumbled

1 tsp dried herbs

salt and pepper

sauce or gravy, mashed
potatoes and freshly cooked
string beans, to serve

meatloaf

Preheat the oven to 350°F/180°C.

Put the bread into a small bowl and add enough water to soak.
Let stand for 5 minutes, then drain and squeeze well to get rid of
all the water.

Combine the bread and all the other ingredients in a bowl. Shape
into a loaf, then place on a cookie sheet or in an ovenproof dish.
Put the meatloaf in the oven and cook for 30–45 minutes until
the juices run clear when it is pierced with a skewer.

Serve in slices with your favorite sauce or gravy, mashed
potatoes, and string beans.

serves 6

1 oz/25 g white bread, crusts removed and torn into pieces

2 tbsp milk

2 cups freshly ground beef

4 tbsp chopped fresh flat-leaf parsley

1 egg

pinch of cayenne pepper

salt and pepper

2 tbsp olive oil

2/3 cup strained canned tomatoes

7 oz/200 g canned chopped tomatoes

1 3/4 cups vegetable stock

pinch of sugar

1 lb/450 g dried spaghetti

spaghetti & meatballs

Place the bread in a small bowl, add the milk, and let soak. Meanwhile, place the beef in a large bowl and add half the parsley, the egg, and the cayenne pepper. Season to taste with salt and pepper. Squeeze the excess moisture out of the bread and crumble it over the meat mixture. Mix well until smooth.

Form small pieces of the mixture into balls between the palms of your hands and place on a baking sheet or board. Let chill in the refrigerator for 30 minutes.

Heat the olive oil in a heavy-bottom skillet. Add the meatballs in batches, and cook, stirring and turning frequently, until browned on all sides. Return earlier batches to the skillet, add the strained tomatoes, chopped tomatoes and their can juices, vegetable stock, and sugar, then season to taste with salt and pepper. Bring to a boil, reduce the heat, cover, and let simmer for 25–30 minutes until the sauce is thickened and the meatballs are tender and cooked through.

Meanwhile, bring a large pan of lightly salted water to a boil. Add the pasta, return to a boil, and cook for 8–10 minutes until tender but still firm to the bite. Drain and transfer to a warmed serving dish. Pour the sauce over the pasta and toss lightly. Sprinkle with the remaining parsley and serve immediately.

serves 4–6

7 oz/200 g dried egg ribbon pasta, such as tagliatelle

2 tbsp butter

2 oz/55 g fine fresh bread crumbs

1¾ cups condensed canned cream of mushroom soup

4 fl oz/125 ml milk

2 celery stalks, chopped

1 red and 1 green bell pepper, seeded and chopped

5 oz/140 g sharp cheese, coarsely grated

2 tbsp chopped fresh parsley

7 oz/200 g canned tuna in oil, drained and flaked

salt and pepper

tuna-noodle casserole

Preheat the oven to 400°F/200°C. Bring a large pan of salted water to a boil. Add the pasta and cook for 2 minutes less than specified on the package instructions.

Meanwhile, melt the butter in a separate, small pan over medium heat. Stir in the bread crumbs, then remove from the heat and set aside.

Drain the pasta well and set aside. Pour the soup into the pasta pan over medium heat, then stir in the milk, celery, bell peppers, half the cheese, and the parsley. Add the tuna and gently stir in so that the flakes don't break up. Season to taste with salt and pepper. Heat just until small bubbles appear around the edge of the mixture—do not boil.

Stir the pasta into the pan and use 2 forks to mix all the ingredients together. Spoon the mixture into an ovenproof dish that is also suitable for serving, and spread out.

Stir the remaining cheese into the buttered bread crumbs, then sprinkle over the top of the pasta mixture. Bake in the oven for 20–25 minutes until the topping is golden. Let stand for 5 minutes before serving straight from the dish.

serves 4

4 swordfish steaks,
about 5 1/2 oz/150 g each

salt and pepper

fresh cilantro and lime
wedges, to garnish

freshly cooked baked
potatoes, corn cobs and fresh
arugula leaves, to serve

for the marinade

3 tbsp rice wine or sherry

3 tbsp chili oil

2 garlic cloves, finely
chopped

juice of 1 lime

1 tbsp chopped fresh cilantro

chargrilled swordfish

To make the marinade, put the rice wine or sherry, oil, garlic, lime juice, and cilantro into a bowl and mix together well.

Rinse the fish steaks under cold running water, then pat dry with paper towels. Arrange the fish in a shallow, nonmetallic (glass or ceramic) dish, which will not react with acid. Season with salt and pepper, then pour over the marinade and turn the fish in the mixture until well coated. Cover with plastic wrap and refrigerate for about 1½ hours.

When the fish is thoroughly marinated, place a ridged cast-iron grill pan over a high heat until you can feel the heat rising from the surface. Lift the fish out of the marinade, place on the hot pan and chargrill for 4 minutes. Turn the fish over, brush with more marinade and chargrill on the other side for another 4 minutes, or until cooked through.

Remove from the heat and divide among 4 plates. Garnish with chopped, fresh cilantro and slices of lime. Serve with hot baked potatoes, corn cobs and fresh arugula leaves.

serves 4

10½ oz/300 g dried pasta of your choice

salt and pepper

2 tbsp olive oil

9 oz/250 g white mushrooms, sliced

1 tsp dried oregano

scant 1¼ cups vegetable stock

1 tbsp lemon juice

6 tbsp cream cheese

1 cup frozen spinach leaves

creamy spinach & mushroom pasta

Cook the pasta in a large pan of lightly salted boiling water according to the package instructions. Drain, reserving ¾ cup of the cooking liquid.

Meanwhile, heat the oil in a large, heavy-bottom skillet over medium heat, add the mushrooms, and cook, stirring frequently, for 8 minutes, or until almost crisp. Stir in the oregano, stock, and lemon juice and cook for 10–12 minutes, or until the sauce is reduced by half.

Stir in the cream cheese and spinach and cook over medium-low heat for 3–5 minutes. Add the reserved cooking liquid, then the cooked pasta. Stir well, season to taste with salt and pepper, and heat through before serving.

serves 4

3 oz/85 g sun-dried tomatoes
(not in oil)

3 cups boiling water

2 tbsp olive oil

1 onion, chopped finely

2 large garlic cloves,
sliced finely

2 tbsp chopped fresh
flat-leaf parsley

2 tsp chopped fresh oregano

1 tsp chopped fresh
rosemary

salt and pepper

3 cups dried fusilli

10 fresh basil leaves,
shredded

3 tbsp freshly grated
Parmesan, to serve

sun-dried tomato sauce with herbs

Put the tomatoes and boiling water in a bowl and let stand for
5 minutes. Remove one third of the tomatoes from the bowl. Cut
into bite-size pieces. Put the remaining tomatoes and water into
a blender and purée.

Heat the oil in a large skillet over a medium heat. Add the onion
and gently cook for 5 minutes, or until soft. Add the garlic and
cook until just beginning to color. Add the puréed tomato and
the reserved tomato pieces to the skillet. Bring to a boil, then
simmer over a medium–low heat for 10 minutes. Stir in the
herbs and season with salt and pepper. Simmer for 1 minute,
then remove from the heat.

Cook the pasta in plenty of boiling salted water until al dente.
Drain and transfer to a warmed serving dish. Briefly reheat the
sauce. Pour over the pasta, then add the basil and toss well to
mix. Sprinkle with the Parmesan and serve at once.

Divine Dining

serves 4

4 skinless, boneless chicken breasts, about 1 lb 12 oz/ 800 g in total

1 tbsp olive oil

green salad and crusty bread, to serve

for the red pesto

4 1/2 oz/125 g sun-blush tomatoes in oil (drained weight), chopped

2 garlic cloves, crushed

4 tbsp pine nuts, lightly toasted, plus extra for sprinkling

2/3 cup extra-virgin olive oil

roasted chicken with sun-blush tomato pesto

Preheat the oven to 400°F/200°C. To make the red pesto, put the sun-blush tomatoes, garlic, 4 tablespoons of the pine nuts, and oil into a food processor and process to a coarse paste.

Arrange the chicken in a large, ovenproof dish or roasting pan. Brush each breast with the oil, then place a tablespoon of red pesto over each breast. Using the back of a spoon, spread the pesto so that it covers the top of each breast. This pesto recipe makes more than just the 4 tablespoons used here. Store the extra pesto in an airtight container in the refrigerator for up to 1 week.

Roast the chicken in the preheated oven for 30 minutes, or until tender and the juices run clear when a skewer is inserted into the thickest part of the meat.

Sprinkle with the remaining pine nuts and serve with a green side salad and crusty bread.

serves 4

5 cups fresh young spinach leaves

4 oz/115 g cooked ham

4 cups chicken stock

1 tbsp olive oil

3 tbsp butter

1 small onion, finely chopped

1 3/8 cups risotto rice

2/3 cup dry white wine

1/4 cup light cream

3/4 cup freshly grated Parmesan or Grana Padano cheese

salt and pepper

shredded spinach & ham risotto

Wash the spinach well and slice into thin shreds. Cut the ham into thin strips. Bring the stock to a boil in a pan, then reduce the heat and keep simmering gently over low heat while you are cooking the risotto.

Heat the oil with 2 tablespoons of the butter in a deep pan over medium heat until the butter has melted. Add the onion and cook, stirring occasionally, for 5 minutes, or until soft and starting to turn golden. Do not brown.

Reduce the heat, add the rice, and mix to coat in oil and butter. Cook, stirring constantly, for 2–3 minutes, or until the grains are translucent.

Add the wine and cook, stirring constantly, for 1 minute until reduced.

Gradually add the hot stock, a ladleful at a time. Stir constantly and add more liquid as the rice absorbs each addition. Increase the heat to medium so that the liquid bubbles. Cook for 20 minutes, or until all the liquid is absorbed and the rice is creamy. Add the spinach and ham with the last ladleful of stock.

Remove the risotto from the heat and add the remaining butter and the cream. Mix well, then stir in the Parmesan until it melts. Season to taste and serve at once.

serves 4

3 tbsp butter

1 tbsp olive or
sunflower-seed oil

4 boneless rib-eye steaks,
about 8 oz/225 g each

1 garlic clove, finely chopped

8 oz/225 g white mushrooms,
halved or quartered

4 tbsp Madeira or port

salt and pepper

chopped fresh parsley,
to garnish

new potatoes and roasted
vegetables, to serve

rib-eye steaks with mushrooms

Melt the butter with the oil in a large, heavy-bottom skillet over a high heat. When hot, add the steaks, and cook quickly on both sides to seal. Reduce the heat to medium and cook, turning once, for 2½–3 minutes each side for rare, 3½–5 minutes each side for medium, or 5–7 minutes each side for well done. Transfer the steaks to warmed plates and keep warm.

Meanwhile, add the garlic and mushrooms to the skillet and cook, stirring frequently, for 5 minutes, or until softened. Add the Madeira and stir the mixture to deglaze by scraping any sediment from the bottom of the skillet. Season to taste with salt and pepper.

Spoon the mushrooms and pan juices over the steaks and garnish with chopped parsley. Serve at once with new potatoes and roasted vegetables.

serves 8

1 prime rib of beef joint,
weighing 6 lb/2.7 kg

salt and pepper

2 tsp dry English mustard

3 tbsp all-purpose flour

1¼ cups red wine

1¼ cups beef stock

2 tsp Worcestershire sauce
(optional)

Yorkshire pudding and
a selection of vegetables,
to serve (optional)

roast beef

Preheat the oven to 450°F/230°C. Season the meat to taste with salt and pepper. Rub in the mustard and 1 tablespoon of the flour.

Place the meat in a roasting pan large enough to hold it comfortably and roast in the oven for 15 minutes. Reduce the temperature to 375°F/190°C and cook for 15 minutes per 1 lb/ 450 g, plus 15 minutes (1¾ hours for this joint) for rare beef or 20 minutes per 1 lb/450 g, plus 20 minutes (2 hours 20 minutes for this joint) for medium beef. Baste the meat from time to time to keep it moist, and if the pan becomes too dry, add a little stock or red wine.

Remove the meat from the oven and place on a warmed serving plate, cover with foil, and let stand in a warm place for 10–15 minutes. To make the gravy, pour off most of the fat from the pan (reserve it for cooking the Yorkshire pudding), leaving behind the meat juices and the sediment. Place the pan on the stove over medium heat and scrape all the sediment from the bottom of the pan. Sprinkle in the remaining flour and quickly mix it into the juices with a small whisk. When you have a smooth paste, gradually add the wine and most of the stock, whisking constantly. Bring to a boil, then reduce the heat to a gentle simmer and cook for 2–3 minutes. Season with salt and pepper and add the remaining stock, if needed, and a little Worcestershire sauce, if you like.

When ready to serve, carve the meat into slices and serve on warmed plates. Pour the gravy into a warmed pitcher and take direct to the table. Serve with Yorkshire Pudding and a selection of vegetables, if liked.

serves 4

1 large eggplant,
cut into 16 slices

3 tbsp olive oil

3 large garlic cloves, crushed

1 fresh red jalapeño chile,
seeded and finely chopped

8 lamb noisettes

salt and pepper

fresh cilantro sprigs,
to garnish

for the pesto

1 cup shelled fresh, frozen, or
canned fava beans

1 large garlic clove, crushed

1 tbsp chopped fresh cilantro

1/3 cup extra-virgin olive oil

salt and pepper

1 1/2 tbsp freshly grated
Parmesan cheese

pan-fried lamb noisettes

First make the pesto. If using fresh or frozen fava beans, cook in a pan of lightly salted boiling water for 10 minutes, or until tender. Drain and put into a food processor with the garlic and cilantro. Using the pulse button, finely chop.

With the motor running, slowly pour in the extra-virgin olive oil, ensuring that it is well blended. When all the oil has been incorporated, scrape the pesto into a bowl and add salt and pepper to taste and the Parmesan cheese. Spoon into a serving bowl, cover, and let chill in the refrigerator until required.

Meanwhile, arrange the eggplant slices on a large baking sheet and sprinkle with the olive oil, reserving 1 teaspoon, then sprinkle over the garlic and chile. Let stand for at least 30 minutes.

Preheat the broiler to medium and cover the broiler rack with foil. Arrange a single layer of eggplant slices on the broiler rack and cook under the preheated broiler for 3–5 minutes, turning once, until tender and starting to crisp. Remove and keep warm while cooking the remaining slices and lamb.

Meanwhile, preheat a nonstick skillet over medium heat. Season the lamb noisettes, add to the skillet, and brown on all sides, then cook for 6–8 minutes on each side, or until cooked to your personal preference. Arrange 4 eggplant slices on each serving plate, top with the lamb, and serve, garnished with cilantro sprigs and a spoonful of pesto.

serves 4

4 salmon steaks,
about 6 oz each

fresh arugula, to serve

griddled lemon wedges,
to garnish

for the parsley pesto

2 garlic cloves, coarsely
chopped

1/2 cup pine nuts

3/4 cup fresh parsley leaves,
coarse stems removed

1 tsp salt

1/3 cup freshly grated
Parmesan cheese

1/2–2/3 cup extra-virgin olive
oil, plus extra for brushing

salmon steaks with parsley pesto

To make the pesto, put the garlic, pine nuts, parsley, and salt into a food processor and blend to a purée. Add the Parmesan and blend briefly again. Then add 1/2 cup oil and blend again. If the consistency is too thick, add the remaining oil and blend again until smooth. Scrape into a bowl and set aside.

Meanwhile, preheat the grill to medium. Cook the salmon under the preheated grill for 10–15 minutes, depending on the thickness of the fillets, until the flesh turns pink and flakes easily. At the same time, heat a skillet and griddle the lemon wedges to desired effect.

Transfer the fillets to warmed plates with the parsley pesto and fresh arugula and garnish with the griddled lemon wedges. Serve immediately.

serves 4

1 lb 8 oz/675 g monkfish tail, skinned

4–5 large garlic cloves, peeled

salt and pepper

3 tbsp olive oil

1 onion, cut into wedges

1 small eggplant, about 10^1/$_2$ oz/300 g, cut into chunks

1 red bell pepper, seeded, cut into wedges

1 yellow bell pepper, seeded, cut into wedges

1 large zucchini, about 8 oz/225 g, cut into wedges

1 tbsp shredded fresh basil, to garnish

crusty bread, to serve

roasted monkfish

Preheat the oven to 400°F/200°C. Remove the central bone from the fish if not already removed and make small slits down each fillet. Cut 2 of the garlic cloves into thin slivers and insert into the fish. Place the fish on a sheet of wax paper, season with salt and pepper to taste, and drizzle over 1 tablespoon of the oil. Bring the top edges together. Form into a pleat and fold over, then fold the ends underneath, completely encasing the fish. Set aside.

Put the remaining garlic cloves and all the vegetables into a roasting pan and sprinkle with the remaining oil, turning the vegetables so that they are well coated in the oil.

Roast in the preheated oven for 20 minutes, turning occasionally. Put the fish package on top of the vegetables and cook for an additional 15–20 minutes, or until the vegetables are tender and the fish is cooked.

Remove from the oven and open up the package. Cut the monkfish into thick slices. Arrange the vegetables on warmed serving plates, top with the fish slices, and sprinkle with the basil. Serve at once with crusty bread.

serves 4

8 oz/225 g live mussels

8 oz/225 g live clams

2 garlic cloves, halved

1 lemon, sliced

2^1/$_2$ cups water

4 oz/115 g unsalted butter

1 tbsp olive oil

1 onion, chopped finely

2 tbsp chopped fresh
flat-leaf parsley

1^1/$_2$ cups risotto rice

^{1}/$_2$ cup dry white wine

8 oz/225 g prepared squid,
cut into small pieces,
or squid rings

8 oz/225 g uncooked shrimp

4 tbsp Marsala

salt and pepper

lemon wedges, to serve

seafood risotto

Scrub the mussels and clams, discarding any that are damaged
or that don't shut when sharply tapped.

Place the garlic, lemon, mussels and clams in a pan. Add the
water and cook over high heat, shaking the pan, until the shellfish
open. Discard any that remain closed. Transfer them to a bowl
and strain the liquid into a jug. Make up to 5 cups with water.

Bring to the boil, lower the heat, and simmer gently.

Melt 1 oz of the butter with the oil and cook the onion and half
the parsley over low heat until softened. Stir in the rice until the
grains are coated and glistening.

Stir in the wine until it has almost evaporated. Add a ladleful
of the hot stock and stir until absorbed. Continue cooking,
stirring and gradually adding stock, until the rice is tender and
the liquid absorbed.

Melt 2 oz of the remaining butter in a pan. Add the squid and stir
for 3 minutes; add the shrimps and cook until the squid turns
opaque and the prawns pink. Add the Marsala and boil until the
liquid has evaporated.

Add to the rice, with all the remaining ingredients. Season and
serve immediately with the lemon wedges.

serves 4

12 oz/350 g dried fusilli

3 tbsp olive oil

12 oz/350 g exotic mushrooms, sliced

1 garlic clove, finely chopped

$1^3/4$ cups heavy cream

$2^1/2$ cups crumbled Gorgonzola cheese

salt and pepper

2 tbsp chopped fresh flat-leaf parsley, to garnish

fusilli with gorgonzola & mushroom sauce

Bring a large pan of lightly salted water to a boil. Add the pasta, bring back to a boil, and cook for 8–10 minutes, or until tender but still firm to the bite.

Meanwhile, heat the olive oil in a heavy-bottom pan. Add the mushrooms and cook over low heat, stirring frequently, for 5 minutes. Add the garlic and cook for another 2 minutes. Add the cream, bring to a boil, and cook for 1 minute, or until slightly thickened. Stir in the cheese and cook over low heat, until it has melted. Do not let the sauce boil once the cheese has been added. Season to taste with salt and pepper and remove the pan from the heat.

Drain the pasta and tip it into the sauce. Toss well to coat, then serve immediately, garnished with the parsley.

serves 4

1 eggplant, cut into
1-inch/2.5-cm slices

1 tbsp olive oil, plus extra
for brushing

1 large red or yellow onion,
finely chopped

2 red or yellow bell peppers,
seeded and finely chopped

3–4 garlic cloves, finely
chopped or crushed

1 lb 12 oz/800 g canned
chopped tomatoes

1 tbsp mild chili powder

1/2 tsp ground cumin

1/2 tsp dried oregano

salt and pepper

2 small zucchini, quartered
lengthwise and sliced

14 oz/400 g canned kidney
beans, drained and rinsed

2 cups water

1 tbsp tomato paste

6 scallions, finely chopped

4 oz/115 g Cheddar cheese,
grated

vegetable chili

Brush the eggplant slices on one side with oil. Heat half the oil in a large, heavy-bottom skillet over medium heat. Add the eggplant slices, oiled side down, and cook for 5–6 minutes, or until browned on one side. Turn the slices over and cook on the other side until browned, then transfer to a plate. Cut into bite-size pieces.

Heat the remaining oil in a large pan over medium heat. Add the onion and bell peppers and cook, stirring frequently, for 3–4 minutes until the onion is just softened. Add the garlic and cook, stirring frequently, for an additional 2–3 minutes until the onion is beginning to color.

Add the tomatoes, chili powder, cumin, and oregano and season to taste with salt and pepper. Bring just to a boil, then reduce the heat, cover, and let simmer gently for 15 minutes.

Add the zucchini, eggplant pieces, beans, water, and tomato paste to the pan and return to a boil. Reduce the heat, cover, and let simmer for an additional 45 minutes, or until the vegetables are tender. Taste and adjust the seasoning, if necessary.

Ladle into warmed bowls and top with the scallions and cheese.

4

Sweet Temptations

serves 6

for the pie dough

2 1/2 cups all-purpose flour

pinch of salt

7 tbsp butter or margarine, diced

7 tbsp lard or vegetable shortening, diced

about 6 tbsp cold water

beaten egg or milk, for glazing

for the filling

1 lb 10 oz–2 lb 4 oz/750 g–1 kg baking apples

scant 2/3 cup packed brown or superfine sugar, plus extra for sprinkling

1/2–1 tsp ground cinnamon, allspice, or ground ginger

1–2 tbsp water (optional)

traditional apple pie

To make the pie dough, sift the flour and salt into a large bowl. Add the butter and lard and rub in with the fingertips until the mixture resembles fine bread crumbs. Add the water and gather the mixture together into a dough. Wrap the dough and let chill in the refrigerator for 30 minutes.

Preheat the oven to 425°F/220°C. Roll out almost two-thirds of the pie dough thinly and use to line a deep 9-inch/23-cm pie dish.

Peel, core, and slice the apples, then mix with the sugar and spice and pack into the pastry shell; the filling can come up above the rim. Add the water if needed, particularly if the apples are a dry variety.

Roll out the remaining pie dough to form a lid. Dampen the edges of the pie rim with water and position the lid, pressing the edges firmly together. Trim and crimp the edges.

Use the trimmings to cut out leaves or other shapes to decorate the top of the pie; dampen and attach. Glaze the top of the pie with beaten egg or milk, make 1–2 slits in the top, and place the pie on a baking sheet.

Bake in the oven for 20 minutes, then reduce the temperature to 350°F/180°C and bake for a further 30 minutes, or until the pastry is a light golden brown. Serve hot or cold, sprinkled with sugar.

serves 8–10

butter, for greasing

all-purpose flour, for dusting

8 oz/250 g prepared
shortcrust pastry dough,
thawed if frozen

3 tbsp cornstarch

1 heaping 1/3 cup superfine
sugar

grated rind of 3 lemons

1 1/4 cups cold water

2/3 cup lemon juice

3 egg yolks

2 oz/55 g unsalted butter,
cut into small cubes

for the meringue

3 egg whites

3/4 cup superfine sugar

1 tsp golden granulated
sugar

lemon meringue pie

Grease a 10-inch/25-cm fluted pie pan. On a lightly dusted work surface, roll out the pastry dough into a circle 2 inches/ 5 cm larger than the pan. Ease the dough into the pan without stretching and press down lightly into the corners. Roll off the excess dough to neaten the pastry shell. Prick the base of the shell and chill, uncovered, in the refrigerator for 20–30 minutes.

Preheat the oven to 400°F/200°C. Line the pastry shell with parchment paper and fill with dried beans. Bake on a preheated baking sheet for 15 minutes. Remove the beans and paper, and return to the oven for 10 minutes until the pastry crust is dry and just coloring. Remove from the oven and reduce the temperature to 300°F/150°C.

Put the cornstarch, sugar, and lemon rind into a pan. Pour in a little of the water and blend to a smooth paste. Gradually add the remaining water and the lemon juice. Place the pan over medium heat and bring the mixture to a boil, stirring continuously. Simmer gently for 1 minute until smooth and glossy. Remove the pan from the heat and beat in the egg yolks, one at a time, then beat in the butter. Place the pan in a bowl of cold water to cool the filling. When cool, spoon the mixture into the pastry shell.

To make the meringue, whisk the egg whites using an electric mixer until soft peaks form. Add the superfine sugar gradually, whisking well with each addition. The mixture should be glossy and firm. Spoon the meringue over the filling to cover it completely and make a seal with the pastry shell. Swirl the meringue into peaks and sprinkle with the granulated sugar. Bake for 20–30 minutes until the meringue is crispy and pale gold (the center should still be soft). Allow to cool slightly before serving.

serves 6

for the pie dough

1 cup all-purpose flour,
plus extra for dusting

1/4 tsp baking powder

1/2 tsp allspice

1/2 tsp salt

1/4 cup superfine sugar

4 tbsp cold unsalted butter,
diced, plus extra for greasing

1 beaten egg, plus extra
for glazing

freshly whipped cream or
ice cream, to serve

for the filling

2 lb/900 g pitted fresh or
canned cherries, drained

3/4 cup granulated sugar

1/2 tsp almond extract

2 tsp cherry brandy

1/4 tsp allspice

2 tbsp cornstarch

2 tbsp water

2 tbsp cold unsalted butter,
diced

latticed cherry pie

Sift the flour and baking powder. Add the allspice, salt and sugar. Rub in the butter until the mixture resembles fine breadcrumbs. Make a well, mix in the beaten egg, then gather to a dough by hand. Divide into two balls, wrap and chill for 30 minutes.

Preheat the oven to 425°F/220°C. Roll out the dough into two 12-inch/30-cm circles. Use one to line a 9-inch/23-cm round pie dish.

Stir half the cherries and all the sugar over low heat until the sugar melts. Add the almond extract, cherry brandy and allspice. Make a paste with the cornstarch and water. Stir into the cherries, turn up the heat until it boils and thickens, stirring constantly. Cool, add the remaining cherries, pour into the pastry case and dot with the butter.

Cut the second circle into strips 1/2 inch/1 cm wide. Lay strips evenly across the top in the same direction, folding back every other strip. Lay strips crossways over the original strips, folding back every other strip.

Trim and crimp the edges. Brush with beaten egg. Cover with foil and bake for 15–20 minutes. Discard the foil, and bake for a further 15 minutes, or until golden. Serve immediately with freshly whipped cream or ice cream.

makes 24

1 stick unsalted butter, softened, plus extra for greasing

1/4 cup golden granulated sugar

1/4 cup light soft brown sugar

1 egg, beaten

1/2 tsp vanilla extract

3/4 cup all-purpose flour

2 tbsp unsweetened cocoa

1/2 tsp baking soda

2/3 cup milk chocolate chips

1/2 cup walnuts, coarsely chopped

double chocolate chip cookies

Preheat the oven to 350°F/180°C, then grease 3 cookie sheets. Place the butter, granulated sugar, and soft brown sugar in a bowl and beat until light and fluffy. Gradually beat in the egg and vanilla extract.

Sift the flour, cocoa, and baking soda into the mixture and stir in carefully. Stir in the chocolate chips and walnuts. Drop dessert spoonfuls of the mixture onto the prepared cookie sheets, spaced well apart to allow for spreading.

Bake in the oven for 10–15 minutes, or until the mixture has spread and the cookies are beginning to feel firm. Remove from the oven and let cool on the cookie sheets for 2 minutes, before transferring to cooling racks.

serves 8

for the pie dough

scant 1⁵/₈ cups all-purpose flour, plus extra for dusting

2 tbsp unsweetened cocoa

5 oz/140 g butter

2 tbsp superfine sugar

1–2 tbsp cold water

for the filling

6 oz/175 g butter

scant 1³/₄ cups packed brown sugar

4 eggs, lightly beaten

4 tbsp unsweetened cocoa, sifted

5¹/₂ oz/150 g semisweet chocolate

1¹/₄ cups light cream

1 tsp chocolate extract

to decorate

scant 2 cups heavy cream, whipped

chocolate flakes and curls

mississippi mud pie

To make the pie dough, sift the flour and cocoa into a mixing bowl. Rub in the butter with the fingertips until the mixture resembles fine bread crumbs. Stir in the sugar and enough cold water to mix to a soft dough. Wrap the dough and let chill in the refrigerator for 15 minutes.

Preheat the oven to 375°F/190°C. Roll out the dough on a lightly dusted counter and use to line a 9-inch/23-cm loose-bottom tart pan or ceramic pie dish. Line with parchment paper and fill with dried beans. Bake in the oven for 15 minutes. Remove from the oven and take out the paper and beans. Bake the pastry crust for an additional 10 minutes.

To make the filling, beat the butter and sugar together in a bowl and gradually beat in the eggs with the cocoa. Melt the chocolate and beat it into the mixture with the light cream and the chocolate extract.

Reduce the oven temperature to 325°F/160°C. Pour the mixture into the pastry crust and bake for 45 minutes, or until the filling has set gently.

Let the mud pie cool completely, then transfer it to a serving plate, if you like. Cover with the whipped cream. Decorate the pie with chocolate flakes and curls and then let chill until ready to serve.

serves 6

for the base

4 tbsp butter, melted,
plus extra for greasing

1 cup (about 14 squares)
finely crushed graham
crackers

3 tbsp superfine sugar

2 tsp unsweetened cocoa
powder

for the chocolate layer

1 lb 12 oz/800 g mascarpone
cheese

1 1/2 cups confectioners'
sugar, sifted

juice of 1/2 orange

finely grated rind of 1 orange

6 oz/175 g dark chocolate,
melted

2 tbsp brandy

strips of orange rind,
blanched, to decorate

deep chocolate cheesecake

Grease an 8-inch/20-cm springform cake pan.

To make the base, put the crushed graham crackers, sugar, cocoa
powder, and melted butter into a large bowl and mix well. Press
the mixture evenly over the base of the prepared pan.

Put the mascarpone and sugar into a bowl and stir in the orange
juice and rind. Add the melted chocolate and brandy, and mix
together until thoroughly combined. Spread the chocolate
mixture evenly over the crumb layer. Cover with plastic wrap
and chill for at least 4 hours.

Remove the cheesecake from the refrigerator, turn out on to a
serving platter and decorate with twists of orange rind.
Serve immediately.

serves 8

for the cake

butter, for greasing

4 eggs

1/2 cup superfine sugar

1 cup all-purpose flour, sifted

pinch of salt

for the topping

1¼ cups heavy cream

5½ oz/150 g white chocolate, chopped

2¾ oz/75 g dark or white chocolate, melted, for the chocolate leaves

handful of rose leaves, or other small edible leaves with well-defined veins, washed and dried

white chocolate cake

You will need to start on the topping the day before it is required. Put the cream into a pan over a low heat and bring to the boil, stirring. Add the chocolate and stir until melted. Pour into a bowl, cover with plastic wrap and chill overnight.

To make the leaves, brush the melted chocolate over the underside of the leaves. Arrange, coated sides up, on a cookie sheet lined with parchment paper. Chill until set, then peel away the leaves.

Preheat the oven to 350°F/180°C. Grease and line an 8-inch/20-cm round cake tin. Put the eggs and sugar into a heatproof bowl and set over a pan of barely simmering water. Whisk until thick, remove from the heat, and whisk until cool. Fold in the flour and salt. Pour into the pan and bake for 20 minutes, then cool for 10 minutes. Turn out, discard the lining paper, and let cool.

Cut the cake horizontally in half. Remove the chocolate cream from the refrigerator and whisk until thick. Spread one third of the mixture over one half of the cake and top with the other half, then coat with the remaining cream. Chill for 1–2 hours, decorate with the chocolate leaves and serve.

serves 6–8

for the pie dough

scant 1¼ cups all-purpose flour, plus extra for dusting

3 tbsp superfine sugar

pinch of salt

1 stick unsalted butter, diced and chilled

1 egg yolk

water, for sealing

for the filling

1 lb/450 g ricotta cheese

½ cup heavy cream

2 eggs, plus 1 egg yolk

scant ½ cup superfine sugar

finely grated rind of 1 lemon

finely grated rind of 1 orange

ricotta cheesecake

To make the pie dough, sift the flour, sugar, and salt onto a counter and make a well in the center. Add the butter and egg yolk to the well. Using your fingertips, gradually work in the flour mixture until fully incorporated.

Gather up the dough and knead very lightly. Cut off about one quarter, then wrap in plastic wrap and chill in the refrigerator. Press the remaining dough into the bottom of a 9-inch/23-cm loose-bottom tart pan. Chill in the refrigerator for 30 minutes.

To make the filling, beat all the ingredients together in a bowl. Cover with plastic wrap and chill in the refrigerator until required.

Preheat the oven to 375°F/190°C. Prick the base of the pastry shell all over with a fork. Line with parchment paper, then fill with dried beans and bake blind in the preheated oven for 15 minutes.

Remove the paper and beans and let the pan cool on a cooling rack.

Spoon the ricotta mixture into the pastry crust and smooth the surface. Roll out the reserved pastry on a lightly dusted counter and cut into strips. Arrange the strips over the filling in a lattice pattern, brushing the overlapping ends with water so that they stick.

Bake in the oven for 30–35 minutes, or until the top of the cheesecake is golden and the filling has set. Let cool on a cooling rack before removing the side of the pan. Cut into wedges to serve.

serves 4

¹/₈ cup blanched almonds

¹/₃ cup no-soak dried
apricots

1 piece preserved ginger,
drained

1 tbsp honey

1 tbsp syrup from the
preserved ginger jar

4 tbsp rolled oats

4 large cooking apples

stuffed baked apples

Preheat the oven to 350°F/180°C. Using a sharp knife, chop the almonds, apricots, and preserved ginger very finely. Set aside.

Place the honey and syrup in a pan and heat until the honey has melted. Stir in the oats and cook gently over low heat for 2 minutes. Remove the pan from the heat and stir in the almonds, apricots, and preserved ginger.

Core the apples, widen the tops slightly, and score around the circumference of each to prevent the skins from bursting during cooking. Place the apples in an ovenproof dish and fill the cavities with the filling. Pour just enough water into the dish to come about one third of the way up the apples. Bake in the preheated oven for 40 minutes, or until tender. Serve immediately.

serves 12

for the cake

2 eggs

3/4 cup molasses sugar

scant 1 cup corn oil

1 1/3 cups coarsely grated
carrots

2 cups wholewheat flour

1 tsp baking soda

2 tsp ground cinnamon

whole nutmeg,
grated (about 1 tsp)

1 cup roughly chopped
walnuts

butter, for greasing

for the topping

1/2 cup half-fat cream cheese

4 tbsp butter, softened

3/4 cup confectioners' sugar

1 tsp grated lemon rind

1 tsp grated orange rind

carrot cake

Preheat the oven to 375°F/190°C. In a mixing bowl, beat the eggs until well blended and add the sugar and oil. Mix well. Add the grated carrot.

Sift in the flour, baking soda, and spices, then add the walnuts. Mix everything together until well incorporated. Spread the mixture into a greased and lined 9-inch/23-cm square cake pan and bake in the center of the preheated oven for 40–50 minutes until the cake is nicely risen, firm to the touch, and has begun to shrink away slightly from the edge of the pan.

Remove from the oven and let cool in the pan until just warm, then turn out onto a cooling rack.

To make the topping, put all the ingredients into a mixing bowl and beat together for 2–3 minutes until really smooth.

When the cake is completely cold, spread with the topping, smooth over with a fork, and leave to firm up a little before cutting into 12 portions. Store in an airtight container in a cool place for up to 1 week.